Comprehension Skills

CONTEXT

LEVEL
E

Linda Ward Beech
Tara McCarthy
Donna Townsend

STECK-VAUGHN
COMPANY
A Subsidiary of National Education Corporation

Executive Editor:	Diane Sharpe
Project Editor:	Melinda Veatch
Senior Editor:	Anne Rose Souby
Design Coordinator:	Sharon Golden
Project Design:	Howard Adkins Communications
Cover Illustration:	Rhonda Childress
Photographs:	©COMSTOCK INC. / Tom Grill

ISBN 0-8114-7851-3

7 8 9 0 VP 00 99 98

Using context means learning a new word by looking at the words surrounding it. In this book you will learn new words by looking at the context.

What is context? Suppose you were in a house in the city. If someone told you to get some eggs, you might go to the refrigerator. But if you were on a farm, you might go to the chicken coop to get the eggs. In the context of a city, people think of the refrigerator when they think of eggs. In the context of a farm, people think of chickens when they think of eggs.

What Is Context?

Context means all the words in a sentence or all the sentences in a paragraph. In a sentence all the words together make up the context. In a paragraph all the sentences together make up the context. You use the context to figure out the meaning of unknown words.

Try It!

The following paragraph has a word that you may not know. See whether you can use the context (the sentences and other words in the paragraph) to decide what the word means.

Typhoons develop over warm ocean water. They are made of heavy rains and strong, swirling winds. The winds can reach two hundred miles per hour.

If you don't know what **typhoons** means, you can decide by using the context. This paragraph contains these words:

◆ *Clue:* develop over warm ocean water

◆ *Clue:* heavy rains

◆ *Clue:* strong, swirling winds

◆ *Clue:* winds can reach two hundred miles per hour

Find these clues in the paragraph and circle them. What words do you think of when you read the clues? You might think of *weather*. What other words do you think of? Write the words below:

Did you write *storm* or *hurricane*? The context clue words tell you that a **typhoon** is a kind of storm like a hurricane.

Using What You Know

Below are some paragraphs with words left out. Read the paragraphs. Look at the context. Then fill in the blanks with words about you.

Someday I am going to have a _____ of my own. I will _____ my _____ to _____ .

The player _____ the ball. I _____ towards the _____ as the ball _____ very fast. The ball _____ towards my hand. I _____ the ball.

Someday I am going to be a _____ . I will _____ and _____ all over the country. I will be very _____ , and everyone will know my name.

I once had a friend named _____ . When we were younger, we _____ in the _____ . There we _____ . We heard _____ and saw _____ .

I like to _____ in the _____ . My favorite _____ is _____ . If I had a lot of money, I would buy a _____ .

Working with Context

This book asks questions that you can answer by using context clues in paragraphs. There are two kinds of paragraphs. The paragraphs in the first part of this book have blank spaces in them. You can use the context clues in the paragraphs to decide which words should go in each space. Here is an example:

◆

Henry Ford built cars that everyone could buy. He cut down on the costs of (1) . He passed the savings on to his (2) .

B **1. A.** chatter **B.** production **C.** sleep **D.** winter

    2. A. towns **B.** models **C.** customers **D.** cowards

Look at the answer choices for blank 1. Try putting each choice in the paragraph to see which one makes the most sense. Treat the paragraph as a puzzle. Which pieces don't fit? It doesn't make sense for a car builder to cut down on the costs of *chatter*, *sleep*, or *winter*. You have decided what doesn't fit. The correct answer is *production*, answer **B**. Now try to answer question 2 on your own.

The paragraphs in the second part of this book are different. For these you figure out the meaning of a word that is printed in **dark letters** in the paragraph. Here is an example:

◆

The scientists studied the volcano carefully. There was a lump on its side. The lump was getting bigger. They knew that the volcano would **erupt** soon. They warned all the people who lived nearby to move before it blew up.

In this paragraph the word in dark type is **erupt**. Find the context clues, and treat the paragraph as a puzzle. Then choose a word that means the same as **erupt**.

    3. In this paragraph the word **erupt** means

      A. disappear **C.** blow up
      B. get bigger **D.** bring rain

To check your answers, turn to page 62.

How to Use This Book

This book has 25 units. In units 1 through 12, you will read stories with blank spaces where words have been left out. Use the context of each story to help you choose words to fill the blanks. In units 13 through 25, the stories have words printed in dark letters. Use the context of each story to help you choose the correct meaning for the word in dark letters.

When you finish reading each story and answering the questions about it, check your answers by looking at pages 59 through 61. Write the number of correct answers in the score box at the top of the page. After you finish all the stories, work through "Think and Apply" on pages 56 through 58. The answers to those questions are on page 62.

Hints for Better Reading

◆ Look for context clues while you are reading the stories. Ask yourself, Where is this story happening? Who is in the story? What is the story about?

◆ When you finish reading, look at each answer choice carefully. Try to put each answer choice into the paragraph. Remember that the paragraph is like a puzzle. Which words don't fit? Which one fits best?

◆ If you cannot find the answer the first time, look back at the story. Then try the answer choices again.

Challenge Yourself

Read each story and choose the correct answer. Then try to write sentences of your own using the correct answer choices.

Unit 1

The great blue whale is bigger than the dinosaurs were. A human being could stand up straight inside the whale's __(1)__ mouth. However, the whale's throat is very tiny. The whale could not __(2)__ a person.

_____ 1. **A.** little **B.** tremendous **C.** hungry **D.** tight

_____ 2. **A.** taste **B.** capture **C.** swallow **D.** find

The game of tennis began around eight hundred years ago. Players in France hit a ball over a net. However, they did not use a __(3)__ to play the game. They used the __(4)__ of their hands.

_____ 3. **A.** mask **B.** motor **C.** trap **D.** racket

_____ 4. **A.** palms **B.** nets **C.** riddles **D.** families

Your fingerprints are unlike those of any other person. Even twins have fingerprints that __(5)__ . Experts say that fingerprints are the best way to __(6)__ someone. These prints can help solve crimes.

_____ 5. **A.** whisk **B.** vary **C.** flicker **D.** advance

_____ 6. **A.** huddle **B.** invite **C.** grasp **D.** identify

Scientists say that black holes __(7)__ in space, although they cannot be seen. It is thought that black holes __(8)__ when huge stars cave in. If the sun became a black hole, it would be only four miles across.

_____ 7. **A.** budge **B.** gust **C.** exist **D.** lend

_____ 8. **A.** leak **B.** satisfy **C.** admire **D.** develop

People and dolphins have a special __(9)__ . In ancient times people in Greece and Rome included dolphins in their art and stories. Dolphins have been trained in our __(10)__ to do tricks. They even work well with people in experiments.

_____ 9. **A.** relationship   **B.** fortune   **C.** trip   **D.** umpire

_____ 10. **A.** camera   **B.** century   **C.** instants   **D.** lodge

An English boy found a very __(11)__ stamp. In fact, it is the only one of its kind! The boy didn't know the __(12)__ of the stamp. He sold it for $1.50. Today a stamp collector would pay $85,000 for this stamp.

_____ 11. **A.** steep   **B.** split   **C.** rare   **D.** wise

_____ 12. **A.** weight   **B.** value   **C.** grade   **D.** shade

Some people think that lightning will not strike twice in the same place. This __(13)__ is not based on fact. In an electrical storm, a tree, a chimney, or other tall __(14)__ may be hit again and again by lightning.

_____ 13. **A.** middle   **B.** belief   **C.** nation   **D.** cause

_____ 14. **A.** tale   **B.** stream   **C.** object   **D.** sport

Men in the 1300s wore shoes that had __(15)__ long toes. The toes were attached to the knees of their clothes with a chain. This kept the men from falling over their own feet! At that time being __(16)__ could also be dangerous!

_____ 15. **A.** deeply   **B.** extremely   **C.** lowly   **D.** strongly

_____ 16. **A.** dark   **B.** polite   **C.** soft   **D.** stylish

Unit 2

Florida is on the southeastern coast of the United States. It has water on three sides. Since the __(1)__ is warm, there are many palm trees. There are also many beautiful beaches. For these reasons, many people __(2)__ in Florida.

_____ **1.** **A.** climate   **B.** size   **C.** rowboat   **D.** insect

_____ **2.** **A.** water   **B.** test   **C.** vacation   **D.** list

The first motion pictures were made in 1887. To see these movies, people looked through a hole in a box. Movies were later shown on a __(3)__ . Recordings were used for sound. Later, sound was put __(4)__ on the movie film.

_____ **3.** **A.** screen   **B.** oven   **C.** hive   **D.** tub

_____ **4.** **A.** sadly   **B.** happily   **C.** directly   **D.** angrily

Artists often use colors to __(5)__ feelings. Bright colors show happy feelings. Dark colors show sad feelings. When you look at a painting, you can tell what the artist's __(6)__ was.

_____ **5.** **A.** buy   **B.** eat   **C.** shovel   **D.** express

_____ **6.** **A.** height   **B.** mood   **C.** brush   **D.** meal

Nothing lives or grows on the moon. But scientists have discovered that some plants on Earth grow better if they are __(7)__ by the moon. If moon dust is __(8)__ over the plants, they grow much bigger. No one yet knows why.

_____ **7.** **A.** melted   **B.** aided   **C.** wet   **D.** arranged

_____ **8.** **A.** trusted   **B.** curved   **C.** sprinkled   **D.** chosen

Our lives are filled with printed words. Books, newspapers, and __(9)__ use print. We buy __(10)__ that have information printed on them. Paper money is printed. TV uses print. Even games use printed words.

_____ 9. **A.** shoes   **B.** pictures   **C.** magazines   **D.** faces

_____ 10. **A.** songs   **B.** stars   **C.** products   **D.** noise

---

Fishing is one of the most popular sports. You need special fishing __(11)__ if you want to fish seriously. Most experts use a rod that is strong but __(12)__ so it won't break.

_____ 11. **A.** types   **B.** tackle   **C.** news   **D.** bowls

_____ 12. **A.** weak   **B.** famous   **C.** open   **D.** flexible

---

Certain walking races are called the "heel and toe." People walking in such races use a special __(13)__ . They take very long __(14)__ . A heel-and-toe expert can walk one mile in six and one-half minutes.

_____ 13. **A.** technique   **B.** sink   **C.** fort   **D.** table

_____ 14. **A.** strides   **B.** lines   **C.** pencils   **D.** sounds

---

Washington, D.C., was planned by George Washington. It became the __(15)__ of the United States in 1800. Today many people live in the city. But many more people live in the __(16)__ and travel to the city each day to work.

_____ 15. **A.** library   **B.** chair   **C.** war   **D.** capital

_____ 16. **A.** cars   **B.** suburbs   **C.** machines   **D.** farms

Red Jacket was a famous Native American in the 1700s. He helped the British soldiers. He __(1)__ the Americans fighting against the British. A British __(2)__ gave him a red jacket. That is how he got his name.

_____ **1.** **A.** loved   **B.** rewarded   **C.** forgot   **D.** opposed

_____ **2.** **A.** tea   **B.** officer   **C.** rifle   **D.** coat

Experts say that swimming is the best exercise. Swimming __(3)__ your strength. Pushing your way through the water builds your muscles. This exercise is less __(4)__ than most other sports. Swimmers are not hurt as often as are joggers and runners.

_____ **3.** **A.** fails   **B.** tickles   **C.** improves   **D.** poisons

_____ **4.** **A.** dangerous   **B.** correct   **C.** lazy   **D.** awake

Several things help broken bones get well fast. Young people seem to __(5)__ faster than old people do. So the age of the __(6)__ counts. It also helps to get the hurt person to a doctor as soon as possible.

_____ **5.** **A.** yawn   **B.** level   **C.** heal   **D.** bend

_____ **6.** **A.** chapter   **B.** sheet   **C.** doctor   **D.** patient

When roads were built, people threw dirt from each side of the road to the __(7)__ . This raised road came to be __(8)__ a highway.

_____ **7.** **A.** center   **B.** witch   **C.** apron   **D.** contest

_____ **8.** **A.** parked   **B.** swept   **C.** showered   **D.** termed

Rachel Carson was __(9)__ about poisons in the water. She wrote a book saying that the poisons used to kill insects could also kill birds and fish. But the problem didn't stop there. There was a __(10)__ that human food supplies might also be poisoned.

_____ **9.** **A.** harmed   **B.** worried   **C.** proud   **D.** merry

_____ **10.** **A.** possibility   **B.** husband   **C.** farmer   **D.** close

---

A walking catfish can move over dry land when its pond dries up. It has __(11)__ for breathing underwater, but it can also breathe on land. This fish uses its tail to push itself along the ground. It uses its strong __(12)__ to lift the front part of its body.

_____ **11.** **A.** bags   **B.** engines   **C.** claws   **D.** gills

_____ **12.** **A.** eyes   **B.** nose   **C.** fins   **D.** clock

---

To make one __(13)__ , or 2,000 pounds, of new paper, 17 trees must be chopped down. __(14)__ forests are cut down each year because so much paper is needed.

_____ **13.** **A.** plant   **B.** dime   **C.** ton   **D.** mouse

_____ **14.** **A.** Entire   **B.** Happy   **C.** Stolen   **D.** Half

---

Your tongue says several things about your health. The color shows if __(15)__ or heart trouble is present. If your tongue is __(16)__ or it burns, you may have a problem with eating some foods. So don't stick out your tongue at your enemy. Save it for the doctor!

_____ **15.** **A.** language   **B.** fruit   **C.** disease   **D.** jam

_____ **16.** **A.** sore   **B.** late   **C.** plain   **D.** smart

In 1721 the __(1)__ of China declared a special holiday. He called it the Festival of Old Men. Men from all over the country came to the palace. The ruler gave __(2)__ of rice and beautiful pieces of silk to all men over ninety years old.

_____ 1. **A.** cousin **B.** sailor **C.** emperor **D.** player

_____ 2. **A.** bushels **B.** paths **C.** harbors **D.** pillows

Bill Steed started an __(3)__ called Croaker College. The pupils in the school are frogs! Steed teaches the frogs to jump fast. Then they are __(4)__ and ready to enter jumping-frog contests.

_____ 3. **A.** institution **B.** airport **C.** island **D.** army

_____ 4. **A.** jumped **B.** gasped **C.** primed **D.** alarmed

A small animal can __(5)__ us with its movements. For example a hummingbird can fly straight up like a helicopter. It can also fly backwards. A flea can jump one hundred times its own height. If people could do that, they could __(6)__ as high as a forty-story building.

_____ 5. **A.** kid **B.** astonish **C.** judge **D.** hit

_____ 6. **A.** fall **B.** climb **C.** leap **D.** grow

Saint Bernard dogs were used to __(7)__ mountain paths covered with snow. These dogs were trained to __(8)__ people who got lost in snowstorms. In the 1880s a dog named Barry saved more than forty travelers from freezing to death.

_____ 7. **A.** ski **B.** hide **C.** patrol **D.** freeze

_____ 8. **A.** rescue **B.** chase **C.** teach **D.** trick

The Statue of Liberty was __(9)__ in 210 separate pieces. The pieces were packed in __(10)__. Then they were shipped from France to America. There the pieces were joined to form Miss Liberty.

_____ **9.** **A.** whole   **B.** originally   **C.** never   **D.** bent

_____ **10.** **A.** beds   **B.** nickels   **C.** lights   **D.** crates

The first kites were made about 2,500 years ago in China. They were made of large leaves. String had not been __(11)__ yet. The kite strings were made of twisted __(12)__.

_____ **11.** **A.** shown   **B.** liked   **C.** wanted   **D.** invented

_____ **12.** **A.** vines   **B.** trees   **C.** tops   **D.** rows

Some people are __(13)__ that mice scare elephants. But these big beasts do not __(14)__ fear when they see a mouse. However, elephants will run away from a rabbit or a dog.

_____ **13.** **A.** clear   **B.** comfortable   **C.** hopeful   **D.** convinced

_____ **14.** **A.** enjoy   **B.** choose   **C.** exhibit   **D.** challenge

Columbus found many __(15)__ things to eat in the New World. When he went back to Europe, he carried some of these new foods with him. He gave the king and queen of Spain a __(16)__. He offered them corn, peppers, pineapples, pumpkins, and sweet potatoes.

_____ **15.** **A.** hidden   **B.** secret   **C.** short   **D.** delicious

_____ **16.** **A.** banquet   **B.** carpet   **C.** princess   **D.** batter

Before the days of television, kids came home from school and listened to the radio. They liked __(1)__ such as Jack Armstrong and Captain Midnight. These radio programs were produced by food companies. Listeners could send in the tops of __(2)__ boxes and win prizes.

_____ **1.** **A.** ladies   **B.** characters   **C.** scenes   **D.** fences

_____ **2.** **A.** arrow   **B.** circus   **C.** shirt   **D.** cereal

---

Chicago is known as the windy city. People there often __(3)__ about the high winds. Yet __(4)__ to the United States Weather Bureau, Chicago is not that windy. Fifteen United States cities are windier.

_____ **3.** **A.** shake   **B.** race   **C.** comment   **D.** record

_____ **4.** **A.** according   **B.** blasting   **C.** dropping   **D.** blowing

---

No snake can fly. But one snake in India can __(5)__ a short distance. It floats down through the air from one branch of a tree to a branch that is __(6)__ it.

_____ **5.** **A.** glide   **B.** swim   **C.** crawl   **D.** throw

_____ **6.** **A.** over   **B.** beneath   **C.** above   **D.** between

---

An old tale says that if you dig a hole where the rainbow ends, you will find a pot of gold. No one knows where this __(7)__ began. To this day, people who have __(8)__ goals are called rainbow chasers.

_____ **7.** **A.** money   **B.** weather   **C.** kettle   **D.** legend

_____ **8.** **A.** simple   **B.** unrealistic   **C.** national   **D.** reached

Some animals travel great __(9)__ . The humpback whale makes a __(10)__ between two oceans. It travels eight thousand miles. A bird called the wandering albatross circles the world from west to east. It makes a flight of twenty thousand miles.

_____ **9.** **A.** floods   **B.** flights   **C.** distances   **D.** stairs

_____ **10.** **A.** ladder   **B.** chain   **C.** bridge   **D.** voyage

The planet Jupiter has a __(11)__ called the Great Red Spot. This spot is a huge storm. The Pacific Ocean could fit in Jupiter's giant __(12)__ .

_____ **11.** **A.** buggy   **B.** paper   **C.** feature   **D.** hero

_____ **12.** **A.** whirlwind   **B.** color   **C.** earth   **D.** sun

The White House was built of Virginia freestone. This __(13)__ is light gray in color. The White House __(14)__ gray until the British burned it in 1814. After that, the famous house was painted white.

_____ **13.** **A.** state   **B.** siren   **C.** material   **D.** sound

_____ **14.** **A.** mixed   **B.** finished   **C.** remained   **D.** hated

Maria Montessori taught young children how to read, write, and count. These children had never before been __(15)__ . But Maria believed that children discover their own __(16)__ interests. She thought that all children love to learn.

_____ **15.** **A.** public   **B.** riders   **C.** crowded   **D.** successful

_____ **16.** **A.** natural   **B.** memory   **C.** honor   **D.** double

Unit 6

The first Olympic games were held in Greece. Boys between the ages of 12 and 17 entered the junior __(1)__ . At the age of 18, they could enter the __(2)__ contests.

_____ **1.** **A.** schools   **B.** darkness   **C.** events   **D.** grounds

_____ **2.** **A.** small   **B.** championship   **C.** fast   **D.** strange

---

Some bats have only one baby at a time. When the mother bat flies out at night, she carries her __(3)__ along with her. The young one hangs onto the mother as she __(4)__ through the dark.

_____ **3.** **A.** amount   **B.** sister   **C.** newborn   **D.** enemy

_____ **4.** **A.** swoops   **B.** blinks   **C.** motions   **D.** hatches

---

Plants need light in order to grow. But many plants __(5)__ to grow fast in the dark. Corn is one __(6)__ . It grows most quickly during warm summer nights.

_____ **5.** **A.** continue   **B.** burn   **C.** complete   **D.** dip

_____ **6.** **A.** flower   **B.** field   **C.** example   **D.** weed

---

On the __(7)__ person's head, there are about one hundred thousand hairs. When people are young, their hair grows fast. It grows about one hundredth of an inch a day. This __(8)__ growth slows down as people get older. If you never cut your hair in your life, it might grow to be 25 feet long.

_____ **7.** **A.** neat   **B.** old   **C.** average   **D.** noisy

_____ **8.** **A.** hard   **B.** rapid   **C.** sleepy   **D.** straight

There are fifty states in the United States. Alaska and Hawaii __(9)__ no states at all. Maine touches only one other state. Both Missouri and Tennessee are __(10)__ by eight other states.

_____ **9.** **A.** defend   **B.** border   **C.** cross   **D.** show

_____ **10.** **A.** covered   **B.** owned   **C.** held   **D.** surrounded

On April Fool's Day, some people make __(11)__ calls to zoos. So, many zoos unplug their telephones. The zoo workers are busy. They can't __(12)__ time taking messages for Mr. Fish, Mrs. Bear, and Miss Lion!

_____ **11.** **A.** helpful   **B.** ridiculous   **C.** beautiful   **D.** new

_____ **12.** **A.** hurry   **B.** tell   **C.** waste   **D.** count

Young Mozart never went to school. His father __(13)__ him in music and math at home. By the time he was five, Mozart was writing his own music for the piano. A year later he played his __(14)__ for people all over Europe.

_____ **13.** **A.** tried   **B.** found   **C.** paid   **D.** tutored

_____ **14.** **A.** compositions   **B.** lanes   **C.** lessons   **D.** ideas

You have probably heard about people who __(15)__ stamps, signs, strings, buttons, or fire hats. You never know what __(16)__ and silly things people want to save.

_____ **15.** **A.** collect   **B.** carve   **C.** manage   **D.** return

_____ **16.** **A.** tough   **B.** cool   **C.** unusual   **D.** lively

Unit 7

During World War I, many French soldiers carried a doll named Tintin in their pockets. The doll was supposed to bring good __(1)__. Later, *Tintin* became the name of a French comic-book hero. This doll also provided the __(2)__ for the name of Rin Tin Tin, the movie dog.

_____ 1. **A.** shadows   **B.** time   **C.** games   **D.** luck

_____ 2. **A.** cheer   **B.** basis   **C.** treat   **D.** slide

People enjoy all kinds of __(3)__ jokes and riddles. One form of __(4)__ is a pun. A pun is a play on words. For instance, "Why can't a bike go as fast as a car?" The answer is, "Because it's two-tired (too tired)."

_____ 3. **A.** hilarious   **B.** careless   **C.** greedy   **D.** rainy

_____ 4. **A.** building   **B.** humor   **C.** music   **D.** dancing

In many cities ginkgo trees line the streets and __(5)__. This kind of tree is very old. There were ginkgo trees back in the days when dinosaurs __(6)__ the earth.

_____ 5. **A.** metal   **B.** avenues   **C.** trucks   **D.** blades

_____ 6. **A.** caught   **B.** began   **C.** roamed   **D.** copied

The United States Post Office puts __(7)__ of famous people on stamps. The first woman shown on a United States __(8)__ stamp was Queen Isabella of Spain. That was in 1893. In 1902 an American woman appeared on a stamp. She was Martha Washington.

_____ 7. **A.** portraits   **B.** glue   **C.** mirrors   **D.** addresses

_____ 8. **A.** pretend   **B.** sausage   **C.** postage   **D.** rubber

There is only one kind of insect that is __(9)__ to live over the ocean. This insect is a type of water strider. It lays its eggs on the backs of snails and on the seaweed that drifts with the __(10)__ .

_____ **9.** **A.** warned **B.** equipped **C.** ringing **D.** written

_____ **10.** **A.** wind **B.** ship **C.** tide **D.** offer

---

You may see a *herd* of horses or cattle in a __(11)__ . You might see a *warren* of rabbits, a *sleuth* of bears, or a *skulk* of foxes in a __(12)__ . The names *warren, sleuth,* and *skulk* are not as commonly used as *herd.*

_____ **11.** **A.** pasture **B.** city **C.** pond **D.** house

_____ **12.** **A.** hospital **B.** thicket **C.** trailer **D.** station

---

A teacher and writer named Katherine Lee Bates climbed to the top of Pikes Peak. She was very __(13)__ with the beautiful scene she saw from the top of the mountain. She was __(14)__ to write the words for a new song, "America the Beautiful."

_____ **13.** **A.** broken **B.** impressed **C.** lonely **D.** ready

_____ **14.** **A.** inspired **B.** teased **C.** trapped **D.** ruined

---

In ancient Rome people met at city squares. These squares were __(15)__ where roads met and were called *trivium.* At the trivium people talked and __(16)__ bits of news. These unimportant facts became known as *trivia.*

_____ **15.** **A.** rude **B.** sides **C.** located **D.** empty

_____ **16.** **A.** afforded **B.** lied **C.** rumbled **D.** exchanged

Unit 8

Dragons still live. The Komodo dragon in Asia is the largest living __(1)__ . It grows to be over ten feet long. It has a long tail, __(2)__ skin, and a wide red mouth.

_____ **1.** **A.** western **B.** visitor **C.** puppet **D.** lizard

_____ **2.** **A.** thirsty **B.** sweet **C.** rough **D.** private

Exercise can help people live longer. __(3)__ say that people who walk or run about half an hour each day stay in better __(4)__ . Some people say they don't have time to work out. They should take the time. For each hour a person exercises, that person may live an hour longer.

_____ **3.** **A.** Owners **B.** Elephants **C.** Experts **D.** Uncles

_____ **4.** **A.** sunshine **B.** order **C.** matter **D.** health

A woman said to a friend, "Yesterday I fell over forty feet." The friend __(5)__ , "That's just __(6)__ ! Were you hurt?" The first woman said, "No, I was just finding my seat at the movies."

_____ **5.** **A.** felt **B.** exclaimed **C.** discovered **D.** bounced

_____ **6.** **A.** horrible **B.** favor **C.** silent **D.** aboard

Some gardeners like to __(7)__ huge vegetables. A man in New England raised two giant __(8)__ for Halloween. Each one weighed 580 pounds!

_____ **7.** **A.** cultivate **B.** pet **C.** rake **D.** believe

_____ **8.** **A.** ghosts **B.** feasts **C.** pumpkins **D.** cats

Hogs are really very smart animals that like to keep clean. But hogs have no __(9)__ in their thick skin to keep them cool. So they like to __(10)__ in mud.

_____   **9.** **A.** reason   **B.** squeal   **C.** glands   **D.** laws

_____   **10.** **A.** fasten   **B.** punish   **C.** follow   **D.** wallow

When parents scold their children about bad habits, the children may __(11)__ with them. The children may try to prove they are "adult" by keeping the bad habit. It would work better if parents __(12)__ their children when they learned better habits.

_____   **11.** **A.** operate   **B.** echo   **C.** limit   **D.** argue

_____   **12.** **A.** congratulated   **B.** answered   **C.** won   **D.** fought

Do you ever snore? The loudest snore on record was made by a man in England in 1984. This snore __(13)__ listeners out of their seats! It was as __(14)__ as the blast of a motorbike starting.

_____   **13.** **A.** granted   **B.** startled   **C.** sank   **D.** helped

_____   **14.** **A.** deafening   **B.** whispering   **C.** quiet   **D.** cozy

The Cummins of Virginia have five children. But they don't have to give five separate birthday parties each year. That's because all five children have the same birthday. Although the children are different ages, they can __(15)__ together. These __(16)__ parties are great fun for all.

_____   **15.** **A.** leave   **B.** cook   **C.** celebrate   **D.** give

_____   **16.** **A.** baby   **B.** combination   **C.** candle   **D.** chocolate

Unit 9

People who collect coins are happy when they find a 1909 penny with the letters *V.D.B.* on it. These __(1)__ stand for Victor David Brenner. That is the name of the man who __(2)__ the coin. These special pennies are very valuable.

_____ **1.** **A.** initials   **B.** words   **C.** signs   **D.** prints

_____ **2.** **A.** lost   **B.** designed   **C.** dropped   **D.** owed

A long time ago, everyone had only one name. Then the leader of China __(3)__ that people should have more than one name. Everyone in China __(4)__ a last name from the words in an old poem.

_____ **3.** **A.** proclaimed   **B.** dreamed   **C.** guessed   **D.** slept

_____ **4.** **A.** said   **B.** left   **C.** selected   **D.** heard

The golden carpet is a plant that grows in a hot, dry place called Death Valley. This plant blooms only in __(5)__ rains. Such heavy rains do not come often to the desert. So the golden carpet blooms very __(6)__ .

_____ **5.** **A.** cold   **B.** boiling   **C.** icy   **D.** torrential

_____ **6.** **A.** often   **B.** soon   **C.** infrequently   **D.** repeatedly

At birth a human child has 305 bones. As the child gets older, many of these bones grow together. The number of bones __(7)__ . By the time the person reaches __(8)__ , he or she has only 206 bones.

_____ **7.** **A.** decreases   **B.** showers   **C.** breaks   **D.** weighs

_____ **8.** **A.** adventure   **B.** base   **C.** bottom   **D.** maturity

In the days of ancient Rome, soldiers had to pass an eyesight test. To show that he could see well, a soldier had to look hard, then point to a star named Alcor in the Big Dipper __(9)__ . This star is very __(10)__ and hard to see.

_____ **9.** **A.** glass   **B.** light   **C.** constellation   **D.** command

_____ **10.** **A.** indistinct   **B.** large   **C.** clear   **D.** fancy

---

Perhaps the most difficult breath a person takes is the very first one. A newborn baby's lungs are flat and filled with liquid. The baby must __(11)__ with great force to make its lungs start working. The baby must __(12)__ its lungs with air.

_____ **11.** **A.** inhale   **B.** kick   **C.** lift   **D.** look

_____ **12.** **A.** roll   **B.** help   **C.** serve   **D.** inflate

---

A cockroach can run in __(13)__ of 14 miles per hour. But it cannot run this fast for long periods of time. The centipede is faster and stronger. Once it reaches __(14)__ speed, this insect runs 24 miles per hour.

_____ **13.** **A.** clocks   **B.** excess   **C.** races   **D.** legs

_____ **14.** **A.** less   **B.** wrong   **C.** maximum   **D.** responsible

---

The first elevator in the Washington Monument was powered by steam. People thought it was __(15)__ to ride in the elevator. Women and children were not __(16)__ to use it.

_____ **15.** **A.** tender   **B.** risky   **C.** tasty   **D.** warm

_____ **16.** **A.** permitted   **B.** attacked   **C.** hired   **D.** pushed

President John Quincy Adams was given money to __(1)__ the White House. With $62 of the money, he bought a pool table. Voters were so __(2)__ that Adams finally paid for the table with his own money.

_____ **1.** **A.** furnish **B.** begin **C.** fly **D.** telephone

_____ **2.** **A.** tired **B.** frightened **C.** upset **D.** playful

---

Some birds live many years. Birds in __(3)__ usually live longer than birds in the wild. Pet swans have lived for fifty years. A pet parrot lived to be seventy. In the wild these birds' chances for __(4)__ would have been much less.

_____ **3.** **A.** traffic **B.** captivity **C.** nests **D.** chimneys

_____ **4.** **A.** escape **B.** behavior **C.** survival **D.** winning

---

Long ago in Hawaii, a soldier played a musical __(5)__ called a machete. The soldier was a small man, and he performed funny __(6)__ while he played. Hawaiians gave the machete a new name. They called it a ukelele. *Uke* means "small," and *lele* means "jumping."

_____ **5.** **A.** band **B.** clam **C.** group **D.** instrument

_____ **6.** **A.** actions **B.** prisons **C.** clowns **D.** laughs

---

When Judge Thurgood Marshall was born, he was __(7)__ Thoroughgood. When he was in the second grade, he decided to __(8)__ his name. He did not like the way it was spelled.

_____ **7.** **A.** stepped **B.** christened **C.** taken **D.** cornered

_____ **8.** **A.** learn **B.** understand **C.** bring **D.** modify

Toys were invented before some tools and (9) were. Toys with wheels have been found in Mexico. Experts (10) that the toys date back almost two thousand years. Yet wheels were not used in Mexico to carry people and goods until much later.

_____ 9. **A.** lands   **B.** workers   **C.** utensils   **D.** meanings

_____ 10. **A.** read   **B.** estimate   **C.** charge   **D.** joke

---

One day in 1652, Governor Winthrop of Massachusetts went for a long (11) in the country. He forgot to take a lunch. All he had with him for (12) was a piece of cheese. Today the place where the governor sat and ate his snack is called Cheese Rock.

_____ 11. **A.** parade   **B.** nap   **C.** swim   **D.** stroll

_____ 12. **A.** friendship   **B.** bait   **C.** refreshment   **D.** freight

---

Years ago some people in Brazil told of a scary (13) called Curupira. These people said Curupira did great (14) . He put his feet on backward. By doing this he tricked people into running toward him instead of away from him.

_____ 13. **A.** monster   **B.** river   **C.** practice   **D.** night

_____ 14. **A.** mischief   **B.** work   **C.** drawing   **D.** writing

---

People used to think that jewels cured (15) . Sick people ground the bright stones into a powder and swallowed it. Only rich people could afford this (16) medicine. But it never really worked. It was actually harmful.

_____ 15. **A.** rings   **B.** illnesses   **C.** bacon   **D.** lumber

_____ 16. **A.** brown   **B.** welcome   **C.** useful   **D.** expensive

There have been many shipwrecks and sea __(1)__ . In 1945 the world was at war. A ship was loaded with __(2)__ who were trying to escape the war zone. One night the ship blew up. All the people were killed.

_____ **1. A.** herds   **B.** airplanes   **C.** sails   **D.** disasters

_____ **2. A.** animals   **B.** actors   **C.** refugees   **D.** guns

An earthquake can cause great __(3)__ waves called tsunamis to build up in the ocean. Many tsunamis travel at 500 miles an hour. They flood islands and cause great __(4)__ .

_____ **3. A.** afternoon   **B.** stone   **C.** tidal   **D.** beast

_____ **4. A.** doors   **B.** destruction   **C.** savings   **D.** joy

An iceboat is designed to travel fast over frozen water. It has three runners and comes to a long, __(5)__ point in front. A sail catches the wind. This special sailboat is __(6)__ in Norway, Sweden, and Denmark.

_____ **5. A.** narrow   **B.** ugly   **C.** dirty   **D.** young

_____ **6. A.** slept   **B.** popular   **C.** flown   **D.** addressed

The first Olympic games were held over two thousand years ago. In those ancient games, winners received __(7)__ made of laurel, olive, or palm branches. Today the prizes are different. Winners get gold, silver, and __(8)__ medals.

_____ **7. A.** wreaths   **B.** bargains   **C.** leaves   **D.** balls

_____ **8. A.** first   **B.** yellow   **C.** heavy   **D.** bronze

Nine tenths of the world's ice is in Antarctica. All of the ice on this huge, bare __(9)__ could bury the United States in a layer two miles thick. The cold air is so dry and __(10)__ that there is no mold in Antarctica.

_____ 9. **A.** box   **B.** garage   **C.** continent   **D.** television

_____ 10. **A.** hot   **B.** pure   **C.** angry   **D.** white

A dog's ears are more __(11)__ than a person's ears. A dog can hear sounds that are high-pitched or far away. A dog can also recognize different __(12)__ sounds. A dog can tell which sound its owner's car engine makes.

_____ 11. **A.** common   **B.** sensitive   **C.** amusing   **D.** weary

_____ 12. **A.** wide   **B.** rich   **C.** damp   **D.** complicated

At the Basketball Hall of Fame, people can see __(13)__ about the history of basketball. Visitors can see Bob Lanier's giant shoes and Kareem's special glasses. There are many other __(14)__ from the game.

_____ 13. **A.** books   **B.** exhibits   **C.** mistakes   **D.** rules

_____ 14. **A.** parts   **B.** goals   **C.** souvenirs   **D.** teams

The Scream Machine is a __(15)__ . It is the world's largest and tallest wooden roller coaster. It is 105 feet high. A trip on it takes only one and a half minutes. The Scream Machine gives its riders quite an amazing __(16)__ !

_____ 15. **A.** lawn   **B.** kitten   **C.** hunter   **D.** marvel

_____ 16. **A.** bath   **B.** walk   **C.** bandage   **D.** experience

Unit 12

In football the judge of every play is the __(1)__ . It is this person's job to decide when a __(2)__ must be given to a player or team that does something wrong.

_____ 1. **A.** safety **B.** referee **C.** coach **D.** yard

_____ 2. **A.** penalty **B.** reward **C.** penny **D.** season

People who fish dream about catching a ten-pound __(3)__ . These fish do not usually get that large. The ones that do are old and smart. It takes much __(4)__ , cleverness, and luck to outsmart such wise old fish.

_____ 3. **A.** boat **B.** worm **C.** boot **D.** bass

_____ 4. **A.** rushing **B.** snow **C.** patience **D.** pay

The New England Aquarium is in Massachusetts. Visitors have the __(5)__ to see how animals live in the water. Some animals thrill __(6)__ by performing in water shows.

_____ 5. **A.** power **B.** opportunity **C.** itch **D.** desert

_____ 6. **A.** pipes **B.** jewels **C.** audiences **D.** holidays

The cockatiel is a bird that looks like a parrot. But it has a __(7)__ of feathers on its head. The cockatiel makes a nice pet because it is __(8)__ and likes to be around people.

_____ 7. **A.** crest **B.** cup **C.** tail **D.** broom

_____ 8. **A.** mean **B.** messy **C.** affectionate **D.** scary

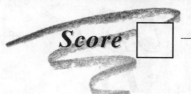
A mountain is worn down year by year. Some of the rocks on the mountain have cracks in them. Water goes into the cracks. As the water freezes, it __(9)__ . This causes the cracks to get larger. Then the rocks are __(10)__ by wind and more water.

_____ **9.** **A.** expands   **B.** replies   **C.** goes   **D.** aims

_____ **10.** **A.** dared   **B.** gone   **C.** seen   **D.** weathered

Deborah Sampson dressed up as a man. She did this so she could join an army __(11)__ during the American Revolution. In one battle she was wounded in the __(12)__ . She removed the bullet herself. That way no one discovered that she was a woman.

_____ **11.** **A.** ax   **B.** regiment   **C.** knife   **D.** park

_____ **12.** **A.** mitten   **B.** suitcase   **C.** rope   **D.** thigh

The unicorn is an imaginary beast. It is supposed to have a __(13)__ horn that twists out of the middle of its forehead. In pictures it is __(14)__ as having the head and body of a horse, the beard of a goat, the legs of a deer, and the tail of a lion.

_____ **13.** **A.** spiral   **B.** buffalo   **C.** button   **D.** flat

_____ **14.** **A.** born   **B.** portrayed   **C.** divided   **D.** touched

Seamounts are __(15)__ cones, or mountains, that rise up from the bottom of the sea. They can be thousands of feet high and still be far below the surface of the water. They are entirely __(16)__ in the ocean.

_____ **15.** **A.** spicy   **B.** awful   **C.** volcanic   **D.** easy

_____ **16.** **A.** killed   **B.** proved   **C.** loose   **D.** submerged

Unit 13

The space shuttle needs extra power to be launched. To get this power, the shuttle is connected to a large fuel **reservoir** and two rocket boosters. These fall off as the shuttle climbs into space.

_____ **1.** In this paragraph the word **reservoir** means
- **A.** card
- **B.** tank
- **C.** lake
- **D.** gas

Many plants grow in places that do not have the minerals they need. The plants must **adapt** to their surroundings. One of these plants is the pitcher plant. It traps and eats insects for the minerals it needs to grow properly.

_____ **2.** In this paragraph the word **adapt** means
- **A.** enjoy
- **B.** answer
- **C.** adjust
- **D.** hatch

Have you ever seen a sea monster? People in northern Scotland believe a sea monster lives in Loch Ness, a nearby lake. Many people have reported seeing the creature. **Observers** say that it has flippers, a hump, and a long, thin neck.

_____ **3.** In this paragraph the word **observers** means
- **A.** police
- **B.** watchers
- **C.** campers
- **D.** doctors

Bedrich Smetana wrote music. When he was fifty years old, he became totally deaf. But he did not let this **check** his interest in music. He wrote some of his finest pieces after going deaf.

_____ **4.** In this paragraph the word **check** means
- **A.** mark
- **B.** nail
- **C.** stop
- **D.** open

The honeysucker, or honey possum, eats the **nectar** found in large flowers. To do this it sticks its long, thin nose into a flower. Then it uses its long, rough tongue to get the sticky food.

_____ **5.** In this paragraph the word **nectar** means

    A. fruit   **C.** sweet liquid

    B. roots   **D.** green leaves

In times long ago, a feast was more than just fancy food on a table. People dressed in fine clothing. Guests were often **entertained** with music, dancing, and juggling.

_____ **6.** In this paragraph the word **entertained** means

    A. starved   **C.** invited

    B. seated   **D.** amused

People have always feared the blasts of hot lava and ashes from a volcano. The power of a volcano has caused many disasters. In 1991 the explosion of a volcano in the Philippine Islands **demolished** an air force base. The base was completely covered with hot ash.

_____ **7.** In this paragraph the word **demolished** means

    A. built   **C.** destroyed

    B. visited   **D.** landed

A boomerang is made so that it returns to the person who throws it. A boomerang has two arms and a **curve** in the middle. This shape makes the boomerang spin. This spinning causes the boomerang to circle back to the person who threw it.

_____ **8.** In this paragraph the word **curve** means

    A. leg   **C.** belt

    B. well   **D.** bend

People who test perfumes train their sense of smell. They can often **distinguish** among ten thousand different scents.

_____ **1.** In this paragraph the word **distinguish** means
- **A.** try harder
- **B.** see a nose
- **C.** get stronger
- **D.** find a difference

Long ago both men and women wore fine clothes made of **lace**. People made this fancy needlework by hand. Women wore dresses, shawls, and even gloves made of it. Men wore it at the necks of their shirts.

_____ **2.** In this paragraph the word **lace** means
- **A.** grease
- **B.** string
- **C.** cloth
- **D.** paint

The month of May is not complete without the **lilac**. People all over the world enjoy the lovely purple of its flowers. It brightens wild fields and city yards.

_____ **3.** In this paragraph the word **lilac** means
- **A.** bird
- **B.** bush
- **C.** color
- **D.** plum

Marco Polo was a famous traveler of long ago. He went from his home in Italy to the far-off land of China. Marco wrote a book about life in China. People in Europe found the book **fascinating**. They were eager to find out more.

_____ **4.** In this paragraph the word **fascinating** means
- **A.** foolish
- **B.** boring
- **C.** regular
- **D.** interesting

The moon appears to change its shape over a period of about thirty days. For that reason the moon can be used to measure the passing of time. That's why people long ago developed **lunar** calendars.

_____ **5.** In this paragraph the word **lunar** means

    A. of the time   **C.** of the moon

    B. of long ago   **D.** of the people

Many people in Mexico take great delight in folk dancing. They wear **jubilant** smiles as they whirl to the lively music. The women wear brightly colored skirts that twirl as they dance.

_____ **6.** In this paragraph the word **jubilant** means

    A. sad   **C.** fast

    B. busy   **D.** joyful

One sign of spring is the sound of tiny peepers. As the nights get warmer, these little frogs call from high in the trees. The **adhesive** pads on their feet help them stay on tree branches.

_____ **7.** In this paragraph the word **adhesive** means

    A. sticky   **C.** loud

    B. oily   **D.** wise

Plants can be attacked by insects or destroyed by bad weather. Sometimes plants are struck by an **epidemic**. Then many plants get sick and die.

_____ **8.** In this paragraph the word **epidemic** means

    A. farmer   **C.** hoe

    B. disease   **D.** climate

Rosa Lee Parks is a **notable** figure in the civil rights movement. She refused to obey the law that said that black people must sit in the back of the bus. She won a medal for her courage.

_____ **1.** In this paragraph the word **notable** means
- **A.** sad
- **B.** important
- **C.** comfortable
- **D.** running

The first telephone in the White House was **installed** in 1877. Rutherford B. Hayes was president then. He ordered the new phone.

_____ **2.** In this paragraph the word **installed** means
- **A.** called up
- **B.** fixed up
- **C.** removed
- **D.** put in

Some people say the wolverine is the most **crafty** animal in the United States. It finds traps in the snow, then it follows the trail to the trapper's cabin. There the animal eats all the food and takes away the pots and pans.

_____ **3.** In this paragraph the word **crafty** means
- **A.** poor
- **B.** mean
- **C.** clever
- **D.** thirsty

Some plants develop seeds. These seeds develop into new plants. Seeds will not **sprout** until conditions are right. The seed must have the right temperature, water, and soil.

_____ **4.** In this paragraph the word **sprout** means
- **A.** break
- **B.** scratch
- **C.** begin to grow
- **D.** begin to die

Many people wear black as a sign of **mourning**. In China the color for death is white. People in Turkey wear purple. But everywhere people follow special customs when someone dies.

_____ **5.** In this paragraph the word **mourning** means
    A. seeing dawn   **C.** showing joy
    B. feeling sick   **D.** showing sadness

The most common **source** of milk is the cow. The goat also gives milk. Other animals that give milk are the camel, buffalo, yak, reindeer, llama, and zebra.

_____ **6.** In this paragraph the word **source** means
    A. bottle   **C.** drink
    B. direction   **D.** supply

When Franz Liszt played the piano, he became **violent**. Often the keys would fly off the piano. Sometimes the strings of the piano would snap with the force of his blows.

_____ **7.** In this paragraph the word **violent** means
    A. rough   **C.** gentle
    B. purple   **D.** large

In 1608 Thomas Coryat brought a new custom to England. He had learned how to eat with a fork. At first the English didn't think this new way to eat was **appropriate**. They did not think it was a good idea. They did not begin to use forks until some time later.

_____ **8.** In this paragraph the word **appropriate** means
    A. fun   **C.** filling
    B. correct   **D.** magic

Some people fear alligators. They need not. There are not many **authentic** cases of alligators attacking people. Most reports have not been backed by facts.

_____ **1.** In this paragraph the word **authentic** means
- **A.** long
- **B.** thin
- **C.** real
- **D.** lengthy

You will find few birds in the deepest, darkest part of a forest. Birds like a **habitat** near the edge of the forest. There is more food for them there.

_____ **2.** In this paragraph the word **habitat** means
- **A.** sunshine
- **B.** place
- **C.** cage
- **D.** insect

You know that the "home on the range" is where the deer and the antelope play. But no animal in North America fit the true **classification** of antelope.

_____ **3.** In this paragraph the word **classification** means
- **A.** friendliness
- **B.** kind of music
- **C.** particular group
- **D.** surrounding land

The **archery** skills of the Native Americans were very good. With homemade bows and arrows, these hunters could kill bison while riding horseback.

_____ **4.** In this paragraph the word **archery** means
- **A.** tracking
- **B.** musical
- **C.** public speaking
- **D.** arrow shooting

Swords were the most important weapons used by knights of old. But when guns were developed, the use of swords **declined**.

_____ **5.** In this paragraph the word **declined** means

    A. grew   **C.** rose

    B. dropped   **D.** rushed

Henry Ford didn't invent the factory, but he improved it. Ford used **conveyors** that brought parts to the workers as they stood in their places.

_____ **6.** In this paragraph the word **conveyors** means

    A. mattresses   **C.** types of small airplanes

    B. skilled workers   **D.** means of carrying things

Astronauts have a big problem when traveling in space. In space, water does not pour. Drops of water just float around. So astronauts must use special **methods** for getting clean. They can't take regular baths or showers. They must wash with special equipment.

_____ **7.** In this paragraph the word **methods** means

    A. brushes   **C.** ways

    B. ideas   **D.** tubs

In spite of its name, banana oil isn't **derived** from bananas. It is made from chemicals that are mixed in a laboratory. The smell of the oil is like the smell of a banana.

_____ **8.** In this paragraph the word **derived** means

    A. taken   **C.** grown

    B. slippery   **D.** pasted

In the middle of Enterprise, Alabama, stands a **monument**. It is shaped like an insect called the boll weevil. This insect once ate all the cotton plants in Enterprise. So people grew peanuts. They earned more money with peanuts. That's why they honored the boll weevil.

_____ **1.** In this paragraph the word **monument** means
- **A.** statue
- **B.** farm
- **C.** tree
- **D.** plant

People build houses for birds called purple martins. Purple martins are welcome because they **devour** insects.

_____ **2.** In this paragraph the word **devour** means
- **A.** deliver
- **B.** admire
- **C.** eat
- **D.** build

The ramp is a vegetable that is like an onion. Although the ramp has an **annoying** smell, people still eat it.

_____ **3.** In this paragraph the word **annoying** means
- **A.** sweet
- **B.** cooked
- **C.** slanted
- **D.** unpleasant

Most animals use some kind of **respiration** to stay alive. A water spider gets air from large bubbles in the water. Whales, on the other hand, must come to the surface of the water to get air for their lungs.

_____ **4.** In this paragraph the word **respiration** means
- **A.** food
- **B.** breathing
- **C.** water
- **D.** trick

When ducks **migrate** south each fall, many of them pass over Stuttgard, Arkansas. So the people there hold a duck-calling contest. As the ducks fly by, the people quack away!

_____ **5.** In this paragraph the word **migrate** means
  A. locate   **C.** travel
  B. mumble   **D.** honk

Have you ever seen a moonbow? It's like a rainbow, but it's made by the moon. Moonbows **occur** when the moon's light shines through the mist from a waterfall.

_____ **6.** In this paragraph the word **occur** means
  A. rain   **C.** happen
  B. flow   **D.** disappear

Once a man checked out a book from a library. He **neglected** to return it. The book was finally returned by his great-grandson 145 years later. Although the fine came to $2,264, the great-grandson did not have to pay it.

_____ **7.** In this paragraph the word **neglected** means
  A. hurried   **C.** borrowed
  B. failed   **D.** remembered

Every June **mobs** of people gather at Jensen Beach in Florida to watch for sea turtles. Hundreds of people snap pictures of the turtles as they lay their eggs.

_____ **8.** In this paragraph the word **mobs** means
  A. crowds   **C.** swimmers
  B. visitors   **D.** couples

Unit 18

Clowns spend much time painting their faces. They don't want people to copy their design. Pictures of the clowns' faces are put in a file as a **permanent** record.

_____ **1.** In this paragraph the word **permanent** means
- **A.** playing
- **B.** pretty
- **C.** lasting
- **D.** broken

A **typical** American saying is *O.K.* There are many stories about how this saying got started. One story is that some writers in Boston were having fun. They used *O.K.* to stand for "oll korrect," a misspelling of "all correct."

_____ **2.** In this paragraph the word **typical** means
- **A.** usual
- **B.** west
- **C.** wild
- **D.** odd

Shirley Temple won an Oscar award for her **performance** in the movie *Bright Eyes.* She was in this movie when she was only six years old.

_____ **3.** In this paragraph the word **performance** means
- **A.** youth
- **B.** sewing
- **C.** acting
- **D.** dinner

The town of Young America, Minnesota, **sponsors** a bed-racing contest each year. People line up all sorts of beds on wheels. Then they roll them down the main street toward the finish line.

_____ **4.** In this paragraph the word **sponsors** means
- **A.** owns
- **B.** wins
- **C.** sells
- **D.** holds

Libraries have **revealed** some interesting facts about books that are returned. One librarian reported that socks were often left in books. Another librarian found a peanut butter sandwich in a returned book!

_____ **5.** In this paragraph the word **revealed** means
- **A.** made known
- **C.** torn down
- **B.** kept hidden
- **D.** laughed at

Lizards have a forked tongue. It has two **functions**. The lizard both touches and smells with it.

_____ **6.** In this paragraph the word **functions** means
- **A.** tests
- **C.** teeth
- **B.** purposes
- **D.** leads

Some animals can **resemble** other things. This helps keep them safe from enemies. For instance, the treehopper looks just like a thorn on a rosebush. Birds may like to eat treehoppers, but they can't find them.

_____ **7.** In this paragraph the word **resemble** means
- **A.** see like
- **C.** look like
- **B.** report to
- **D.** differ from

Rain forests grow where it is warm and wet all year. Thick trees and vines form a high **canopy** over the forest. As a result, little sunlight reaches the forest floor.

_____ **8.** In this paragraph the word **canopy** means
- **A.** cloud
- **C.** capitol
- **B.** covering
- **D.** night

A glassmaker heats sand and chemicals in a large furnace. The hot **compound** becomes a thick liquid. The glass is shaped while it's hot. Then the glass cools and hardens.

_____ 1. In this paragraph the word **compound** means
     A. thread   C. iron
     B. flour   D. mixture

Butterflies have many ways to protect themselves. While certain kinds of butterflies are still caterpillars, they eat harmful plants. The plant's chemicals are stored in the **tissues** of the insect's body. This makes the butterfly taste bad. Its enemies will not eat it.

_____ 2. In this paragraph the word **tissues** means
     A. bones   C. group of cells
     B. blood   D. piece of paper

Each day rain falls on a place in Hawaii. That adds up to almost five hundred inches of rain a year. But a place in India is really **moist**. One year about one thousand inches of rain fell.

_____ 3. In this paragraph the word **moist** means
     A. dark   C. wet
     B. green   D. great

Some cities take their garbage to open dumps. The garbage is spread out on the land and then covered with dirt. But there is less and less land. And the piles of garbage are **increasing**. People must think of ways to make less garbage.

_____ 4. In this paragraph the word **increasing** means
     A. shiny   C. useful
     B. growing   D. shrinking

Monkeys use different noises to **communicate**. They shout to tell other monkeys where they are. Some monkeys make sounds to tell other monkeys to stay away. Another kind of noise scares enemies away.

_____ **5.** In this paragraph the word **communicate** means
    A. notice things   **C.** name things
    B. tell things   **D.** show things

How did astronauts **converse** on the moon? They had to speak over a radio. That's because the moon has no air to carry sound.

_____ **6.** In this paragraph the word **converse** means
    A. talk   **C.** play
    B. weep   **D.** listen

Mexico once owned Texas. But many Texans thought Texas should have its own government. Some Texans got together and wrote new laws for Texas. Then they fought a war to win their **independence**.

_____ **7.** In this paragraph the word **independence** means
    A. boats   **C.** reward
    B. freedom   **D.** game

Pearl Buck was American, but she felt Chinese. She lived in China for almost forty years. She wrote stories about Chinese people. Her **career** as a writer lasted a lifetime. During her life she wrote 110 books about the country she loved.

_____ **8.** In this paragraph the word **career** means
    A. movie   **C.** school
    B. work   **D.** rest

Cat's Cradle did not **originate** with children. This string game started with adults who used string for other reasons. For instance, string traps were once set outside of towns in the Far East. People believed that the strings would catch stray ghosts.

_____ 1. In this paragraph the word **originate** means
     A. end   **C.** begin
     B. continue   **D.** believe

When a sailor crosses the equator for the first time, the other sailors make a big event of it. They dunk the sailor in the water. Wet or dry, everyone has a good time at this **frolic**.

_____ 2. In this paragraph the word **frolic** means
     A. party   **C.** route
     B. ship   **D.** trouble

Long ago, Roman soldiers ate a lot of garlic. They thought garlic would make them **courageous** in war. It was important to them to show no fear in battle.

_____ 3. In this paragraph the word **courageous** means
     A. smelly   **C.** brave
     B. sorry   **D.** weak

Why do wooden stairs squeak? Wood changes size with the temperature. When it's hot, wood gets larger. When it's cold, wood **contracts**. The shrinking wood makes the stairs squeak when it's cold.

_____ 4. In this paragraph the word **contracts** means
     A. gets noisy   **C.** gets colder
     B. gets smaller **D.** gets bigger

Long ago a bride's father gave all her shoes to her new husband. This **indicated** that the father no longer had to care for the bride. Today we keep this custom by tying shoes to a wedding car.

_____ **5.** In this paragraph the word **indicated** means
    A. behaved   **C.** prayed
    B. pained   **D.** meant

The oldest false teeth are almost three thousand years old. They were found on the body of a **deceased** person in an old grave. The teeth were strung together with gold wire.

_____ **6.** In this paragraph the word **deceased** means
    A. dead   **C.** healthy
    B. old   **D.** rich

Sir Robert Peel formed a special police force in London to fight crime. It was so **effective** that other towns started special forces, too. These police officers are now called bobbies, for Sir Robert's nickname.

_____ **7.** In this paragraph the word **effective** means
    A. ragged   **C.** quiet
    B. successful   **D.** proud

The bits of paper thrown during parades are called confetti. This word means "candy." Once people threw candy during **festive** and merry events. Now we throw paper.

_____ **8.** In this paragraph the word **festive** means
    A. worn   **C.** smooth
    B. tasty   **D.** jolly

Unit
21

If you want to lose weight, get in an elevator and push the *down* button. When you ride down, your weight drops, too. It is almost ten percent less than when you are **stationary**.

_____ **1.** In this paragraph the word **stationary** means
   A. tight   C. light
   B. still   D. full

Suppose you need to measure a small object, but you don't have a ruler. If you have a dollar bill, you can get an **approximate** measure. Just remember that a dollar bill is a little over six inches long.

_____ **2.** In this paragraph the word **approximate** means
   A. small   C. crazy
   B. certain   D. close

What word gets the most attention in newspapers? It's the word *free*. People are likely to notice an **item** if they might get something free.

_____ **3.** In this paragraph the word **item** means
   A. big sale   C. house
   B. thing   D. animal

Salt had great value in early times. Roman soldiers were paid in coins made of salt. Their word for this money was *salarium*. So today our word for pay is **salary**.

_____ **4.** In this paragraph the word **salary** means
   A. salty   C. money earned
   B. soldier   D. wars fought

Sometimes an alligator **attempts** to eat something that is too big for it. When the alligator can't swallow the large meal, its eyes begin to water.

_____ **5.** In this paragraph the word **attempts** means
- **A.** tries
- **B.** cries
- **C.** swallows
- **D.** forgets

Many cities are going through a **renewal**. Old buildings are being torn down, and new ones are being built. These changes help to give the city new life.

_____ **6.** In this paragraph the word **renewal** means
- **A.** new hat
- **B.** new start
- **C.** final ending
- **D.** good government

Coins and printed paper are not the only forms of **currency**. Some people trade shells or beads when they buy and sell. In South America, cacao beans were once traded for goods.

_____ **7.** In this paragraph the word **currency** means
- **A.** money
- **B.** jewels
- **C.** winning
- **D.** banks

The honey that bees make is not always **edible**. Honey made from some plants tastes very bad. Honey made from other kinds of plants is actually harmful to people.

_____ **8.** In this paragraph the word **edible** means
- **A.** dangerous
- **B.** sold in stores
- **C.** used by bees
- **D.** good to eat

England has been ruled by **monarchs** for hundreds of years. The youngest was Henry VI, who became king at age one. Queen Victoria ruled the longest. King Henry VIII had the most wives.

_____ **1.** In this paragraph the word **monarchs** means
- **A.** husbands
- **B.** children
- **C.** rulers
- **D.** queens

Some animals **hibernate** all winter. The dormouse makes a snug bed of leaves in the fall. It curls up and doesn't come out again until spring.

_____ **2.** In this paragraph the word **hibernate** means
- **A.** dig
- **B.** sleep
- **C.** carve
- **D.** mend

Most people think of the Sahara Desert as a very **arid** place. But some streams run under the sand. People have dug for water and found fish!

_____ **3.** In this paragraph the word **arid** means
- **A.** dry
- **B.** damp
- **C.** bumpy
- **D.** sharp

How are the words *bora*, *chinook*, and *mistral* the same? They are all words for strong winds that **gust** over different parts of the world.

_____ **4.** In this paragraph the word **gust** means
- **A.** drip
- **B.** dust
- **C.** blow
- **D.** fall

Do you like to hear the **booming** of thunder? Go to a place called Boga. People there hear thunder about 332 days of each year.

_____ **5.** In this paragraph the word **booming** means
- **A.** raining
- **C.** flashing
- **B.** tangle
- **D.** crashing

The elephant has the largest ears in the animal kingdom. This **massive** beast needs them because its body is so big. An African elephant's ears can grow to be four feet across.

_____ **6.** In this paragraph the word **massive** means
- **A.** tiny
- **C.** huge
- **B.** chosen
- **D.** fancy

The Purple Heart is an award given to members of the United States armed forces. It is given to those hurt or killed in **combat**.

_____ **7.** In this paragraph the word **combat** means
- **A.** traffic
- **C.** parades
- **B.** fighting
- **D.** hunting

It is thought that Hanson Crockett Gregory invented the doughnut hole. Long ago, doughnuts had no holes. Gregory thought those doughnuts were soggy in the middle. So he **recommended** that his mother make a hole in one. It cooked better that way.

_____ **8.** In this paragraph the word **recommended** means
- **A.** suggested
- **C.** refused
- **B.** forgot
- **D.** doubted

People are fond of apples. We eat and drink them in many forms. Our **vocabulary** includes apple phrases, too. When things are neat, they are in *apple-pie order*.

_____ **1.** In this paragraph the word **vocabulary** means
- **A.** fruit picked
- **C.** desserts liked
- **B.** words used
- **D.** kitchen cupboard

Poison ivy was a big problem to the first settlers in America. This plant grew wild in Virginia. Everywhere people stepped, they found a poison ivy plant. If it came into **contact** with their skin, they began to itch terribly.

_____ **2.** In this paragraph the word **contact** means
- **A.** guard
- **C.** touch
- **B.** chance
- **D.** paste

A hermit crab **dwells** in the empty shell of a snail. When the crab gets too big, it hunts for another home.

_____ **3.** In this paragraph the word **dwells** means
- **A.** lives
- **C.** robs
- **B.** quits
- **D.** views

John Philip Sousa formed a band in 1892. It soon won **recognition** for its lively march music. Even now people still like to hear the songs that made Sousa famous. One special favorite is "The Stars and Stripes Forever."

_____ **4.** In this paragraph the word **recognition** means
- **A.** races
- **C.** attention
- **B.** songs
- **D.** character

Venus is the planet that comes nearest to Earth. Venus and Earth are also very close in size. Earth is only about four hundred miles larger in **diameter** than Venus.

_____ **5.** In this paragraph the word **diameter** means
    A. space   **C.** distance across
    B. circles   **D.** total weight

At one time people used **vague** words for cooking. They said "a pinch of salt" or a "dash of pepper." In the 1890s Fannie Farmer changed that. She used exact measurements in her cookbooks.

_____ **6.** In this paragraph the word **vague** means
    A. strong   **C.** short
    B. hard   **D.** unclear

The *Mayflower* was a ship that brought settlers to America. It was named after a flower by the same name. This flower **adorned** places on May Day. People put the flowers everywhere for the spring celebration.

_____ **7.** In this paragraph the word **adorned** means
    A. painted   **C.** sailed
    B. decorated   **D.** pictured

The word *Yankee* might have come from the Dutch words *Jan Kees*. This meant "John Cheese." The Dutch people liked cheese. But they didn't think this name was very **flattering**.

_____ **8.** In this paragraph the word **flattering** means
    A. straight   **C.** praising
    B. soft   **D.** delicious

On July 11, 1991, the people in Hawaii had a thrilling experience. The earth, moon, and sun lined up. This made the sun seem to disappear. This **eclipse** of the sun lasted over seven minutes.

_____ **1.** In this paragraph the word **eclipse** means
- **A.** darkening
- **B.** coloring
- **C.** brightness
- **D.** heat

Skin diving is a wonderful way to see what is below the water's surface. Divers wear a mask so that they can see clearly. They also wear fins to help them swim. They breathe through a **snorkel** while floating on the water's surface.

_____ **2.** In this paragraph the word **snorkel** means
- **A.** spray
- **B.** sofa
- **C.** creek
- **D.** tube

Sugar is used to sweeten many foods. Most sugar comes from sugar beets and sugar cane. The sugar is **refined** before it is used. This makes the sugar white.

_____ **3.** In this paragraph the word **refined** means
- **A.** stamped
- **B.** heard
- **C.** moved around
- **D.** made pure

People who are new to camping in the mountains can't **comprehend** why hard-boiled eggs take so long to cook. It is because water boils at a lower temperature in the mountains. The eggs have to stay in the boiling water for a longer time.

_____ **4.** In this paragraph the word **comprehend** means
- **A.** direct
- **B.** turn
- **C.** understand
- **D.** measure

Richard Leakey was born in Kenya, Africa, in 1944. He has found many important **fossils** of early humans. He discovered some skulls that are thought to be over one million years old!

_____ **5.** In this paragraph the word **fossils** means
- **A.** bones
- **B.** robes
- **C.** barns
- **D.** hills

People have long believed that bulls are attracted to the color red. Scientists have **investigated** whether bulls can see colors. They have found that a red shirt doesn't interest a bull any more than a blue one does.

_____ **6.** In this paragraph the word **investigated** means
- **A.** ridden
- **B.** fought
- **C.** danced
- **D.** studied

The Cabinet is a group of **advisers** who help the president make decisions. There are usually 14 members. The president determines who is part of the Cabinet.

_____ **7.** In this paragraph the word **advisers** means
- **A.** families
- **B.** helpers
- **C.** kings
- **D.** knights

Taking care of your teeth is very important. If you don't brush often, you can develop **cavities** in your teeth. These need to be filled by a dentist.

_____ **8.** In this paragraph the word **cavities** means
- **A.** holes
- **B.** candies
- **C.** braces
- **D.** frames

There was a king called Aga Khan III. He was glad he weighed 243 pounds. People had agreed to **contribute** to his birthday party. Their present was his weight in diamonds.

_____ **1.** In this paragraph the word **contribute** means
- **A.** keep
- **B.** weigh
- **C.** give
- **D.** scale

There are 365 steps going up to the United States Capitol building. It's no **coincidence** that there are also 365 days in a year. The steps were made so that there was one for each day.

_____ **2.** In this paragraph the word **coincidence** means
- **A.** joke
- **B.** plan
- **C.** accident
- **D.** change

Long ago there were no buttonholes. Buttons were just for show. They were made of rare metals and stones. Rich people wore them on grand **occasions**.

_____ **3.** In this paragraph the word **occasions** means
- **A.** events
- **B.** crackers
- **C.** rocks
- **D.** trains

The writer Charles Dickens had a cat. The cat watched while Dickens worked on his **novels**. When the cat decided that Dickens had written enough, it put out the candle.

_____ **4.** In this paragraph the word **novels** means
- **A.** rooms
- **B.** books
- **C.** repairs
- **D.** baggage

Early people did not have clocks. So they used other ways to tell time. The Egyptians measured a small amount of time called an instant. An instant was the time it took for a hippopotamus to **survey** a place for danger.

_____ **5.** In this paragraph the word **survey** means
- **A.** load
- **B.** smash
- **C.** ask
- **D.** examine

Thousands of dogs served in the **military** during World War II. Some of these animals were put in parachutes and dropped from planes. When they landed, they carried messages behind the lines.

_____ **6.** In this paragraph the word **military** means
- **A.** forest
- **B.** attack
- **C.** battle
- **D.** armed forces

Peddlers used to sell things from door to door. They carried cloth, clocks, buttons, and knives. Peddlers sang happy songs to **tempt** people to buy things.

_____ **7.** In this paragraph the word **tempt** means
- **A.** scare
- **B.** sell
- **C.** encourage
- **D.** hope

Purple dye was rare long ago. Since it was hard to get, it cost a lot. As a result purple became the **imperial** color. It was used only by kings and queens.

_____ **8.** In this paragraph the word **imperial** means
- **A.** royal
- **B.** inside
- **C.** yellow
- **D.** best

Think and Apply

Word Search

Each of the sentences on this page is missing a word. Read the sentences and choose a word from the box to go in each one. Write the word on the line.

trench	confess	gravity
absent	vicious	laughter
ballot	failure	geography

1. During a thunderstorm there may be a power _____ .

2. The _____ dog had to be chained.

3. The force that holds everything on Earth is _____ .

4. She finally had to _____ her crime to the judge.

5. The soldiers dug a _____ .

6. When someone is feeling sad, _____ may be the best medicine.

7. The study of places around the world is _____ .

8. When you vote, you cast a _____ .

9. If you are not at school, you are counted _____ .

To check your answers, turn to page 62.

Double O in Context

Two *o*'s form a part of many different words. Read the sentences below. One word has been left out of each sentence. Look at where the double *o* is placed in that word. Write letters on the lines to make the correct word.

1. When a plant flowers, it ___ ___ oo ___ ___ .

2. A group of scouts is called a ___ ___ oo ___ .

3. If you work well with others, you are

___ oo ___ ___ ___ ___ ___ ___ ___ ___ .

4. A hat that's connected to a jacket is a ___ oo ___ .

5. Evidence is also called ___ ___ oo ___ .

6. A machine used for weaving cloth is a ___ oo ___ .

7. The ___ ___ oo ___ is the man standing next to the bride.

8. A large North American deer is the ___ oo ___ ___ .

9. The place where a bird rests or sleeps is a ___ oo ___ ___ .

10. An ___ ___ ___ oo is a house made from blocks of ice.

To check your answers, turn to page 62.

Going for the Gold

Read the story. Find the ten words that do not make sense in the context of the story. Draw a line through those words. On the lines below the story, list ten words that would make more sense in the story context.

      Destrie and Ruth packed up all of their possessions and put them into the covered wagon. They hitched the team of seashells to the wagon and headed west. They were jumping to California in doubt of gold. They wanted to strike it loud.

      It was a long, hard meadow across the country. Sometimes Destrie and Ruth stopped at rocks along the way to buy supplies. But most of the time the couple was on the beach.

      When Destrie and Ruth arrived in California, they found some land to eat. Then they mixed themselves a cabin. They searched for gold every day, but they never ran any.

1. _____   6. _____

2. _____   7. _____

3. _____   8. _____

4. _____   9. _____

5. _____   10. _____

To check your answers, turn to page 62.